The Ode of Melby

Natalie Mitchell

BookLeaf Publishing

Presentation by *BookLeaf Publishing*

Web: www.bookleafpub.com

E-mail: info@bookleafpub.com

ISBN: 978-93-95890-16-8

First edition 2022

DEDICATION

This is dedicated to those, I love beyond words and it is dedicated to any and all who were and are a part of my human experience.

ACKNOWLEDGEMENT

Let me start by acknowledging my dad because he has always been supportive of my writing poetry. He also, made sure to send me on trips and help me enter contest as well. My mother because she would allow me to read poetry to her in the wee hours and she checks in to see if I have written often. I must acknowledge my children as well because they lightened up my adventure when composing poetry. My cousin, Love as she too writes and allows me to share my writing journey with her. She also, cheers me on as well and is a great source to pour into. My brother is always saying to write a novel because he sees a story within the poetry. My dear friend, Sean because he's always encouraging me to write. Not forgetting my betroth, as he has been up with me during my typing and obsessing over creating this poetry book. Finally, I would like to thank and acknowledge, He who created me.

PREFACE

In our human experiences, we often find ourselves caught up in the fleeting moments of life. The times where it all seems a bit much and either we gain sound perspective or we are without it entirely. Some of these moments are composed of love, death, fickle emotions, deep seated emotions, and so much more. In here you venture into the perspectives that haunt me still and either bring me joy or heartache, clarity or into fog.

Quill

Hath thou no bones with me
for I am some lone thing
Preach me, a derelict of thy desire

I utter for ye, guttural as the wolf
Yet, there is no propagation, in the night
ye hath to comprehend, silence

For it is no remedy and thou is no, mute
Ye madness whispers to me, yet evades
leaving me parched but engaged

Art thou my muse, alive to but beguile me
my beloved understudy, cast your dirge
I will meet ye there and bury my thoughts

Implore ye, I require verbiage and bondage
bespeak like a murder of crows
maddened shadows and illuminated dark

Dost thou hear thy bard and vagabond
threnodies haunt me and thou escapes
For whatever shall I say, without ye

Thou art my beloved, Quill and verbosity
O how, I miss thee and loathe thee
For what am I, void of thee but nothing

I grasp thee and ye falls silent, blind, deaf
Where is thou ink and vivaciousness
Art ye in some happenstance purgatory

Require I, to write and to die everyday
macabre and love, Moon and Sun
pulchritude and dilapidation

For thou art a Quill, who hath run dry
I am a prisoner without ink and death
We shan't live without the marrow of my bones_

Even our end shall lack luster

Details

As we decipher the minutiae
its murmurs reverberate
through the foundations
of our lives_
Affecting all, intricately

Silent Emote

When there is so much to say but left unsaid
because emotive verbosity falls and fails
miserably before it can effectively reach distant
ears

You emote and I emote but we have differing
vices
and our aliments manifest in different books

Sympathy and empathy are strangers sitting
side by side on public benches_
on savvy leather corporate chairs and decorative
places to geared towards blending on furniture
to general to care

They are as estranged siblings but they share
the same guttural despair_
Human commonality is not enough, not enough
for acknowledgment_
Not enough for a well placed tear and closed
hearts
do not dare adhere

Facades are brilliant like suited mimes but
what of silence and a postured gaze_

They go about like functioning addicts
tinkering by like manufactured dolls_
but their innards are hardly there because a
great emptiness lingers there

Masks tend to fade away_
how do we appropriate that which hinders
our fruit_
That which hinders our gifting_
Where do we lie, when the pain becomes a
vivid neighbor, within a shattered mirror

We Two Entities

I apologize, we two egotistical beings ever laid
eyes upon one another

Potentiality is a well embalmed carcass, when it
lacks vivid purpose

because fallacy driven animation gives it life

Emotive vultures circle in angst of our plight

We live etched in light, where minute dark
rooms
are on hand

And hurried polaroid's paint only the good times

As we embrace, I breath in familiarity
You see

Because noxious stimuli invigorates memories
and I am overcome

By the provided hypothalamus, scents of our
potential

O how they destroy me and bring me life but when did life

Shadow false hope

You vanquish me and welcome me, love me and despise me

but clutch to the carcass of our potentiality and I, visit

Its familiar grave and die with it, over and over again

Perhaps, I should not bring it flowers because they too go without water

I gander, our love is a filed of death but we treat it as our personal garden_

And well, I can smell the ever fragrant posies

Beautiful Tragedy

I recall Woden from the very chasms of my
dreams.
Subsequently, he lurked about like a miniscule
cue
of what is to come

Like a constant melodramatic drumroll and
classically
composed strings of the eighty=eight, timed and
strummed strategically

Like a beautiful tragedy_
Mundane conditions purloined him of his
pulchritude
and deemed him the living death

His very existence, seems a crime, a mere
malady
I ponder upon his purpose and it seems to have
no rhyme
So, I deem him, Poe's Conqueror Worm

Writhing forth, from the depths of affliction_
I picture him grotesque, like dilapidated innards
of foul play

I do not orchestrate, nor comprehend grand
design
I cannot inquire of his actuality, nor shall, I
dwell upon
my neighbors fatality

However, the reality of my disdain rattles the
geranium
coursing through my veins, consciously_
I abstain

Yet, the sub-mind painstakingly, dreams of the
calamities
to which it is framed.

Moments

Whenever, I disassociated things were easier
my drive was grueling but in a way no one
should live

My accomplishments were not felt but followed
behind
fanciful metaphors and rhymes

neatly placed words to paper_

Moments that passed by, only to be rewritten,
revised and
tailored because scattered etching on dead trees

was my only reprieve_

Me, I cannot write myself our of tragedy or
tattered happenings
my pen can no longer hoist up realities

that need to be felt_

Previously it murdered only to recreate, slayed
dragons only
to demonstrate, brought life only to reverberate
and provoked thought, only to animate_

It stood on many fronts, a forgotten quill,
inkblots spill forth
only to reveal, I, me, my innermost burning
candles at many ends

winning, well that depends

I am Poetry

I am poetry in motion,
made of ever progressing particles,
never to stay upon things which shame my heart.
I am a steady movement,
towards grace and all that is good,
because I am a product of wrath and I strive, I
strive
and I, like a capricious wind continue to move
the tufts of floral beauty
and dance with the earthly procession of trees.

I am poetry in motion
confined but never defined,
within the expressive vernacular ushered off of
the faculties of mankind.
I am the voice rattling the cage
and I am the voice of a freed ideology
moving about without the shackles of
manifested strongholds.

I am, motion into thought, propagating without
limits,
like a prayer into the vault of heavenly places.

I am poetry in motion, moving qwerty
keyboard's,
and bic pens

I am a thought
and I am emotion but you dear;
are a victim.
I digress, avidly in likeness with motion because
poetry moves me_
without emotional devotion.

Reflections of the Heart

Verily I spake unto ye
for the heavenly bodies
were clandestine from thee
I hath not even known Spring
until, ye became my Fall

From thine heart to thou soul
lies uncharted canvases
There is a Sovereign Artiste
whom illustrates the emphatic
depth of our love

Even the doves alight and
fathom unblemished freedom there
There, from whence the fields
yield bouquets of blooming promises

Hath thou ever pondered
thy lyrist
O how thy quill, spake unto
sky and Moon
I bequeath unto ye

Thou kiss defied all reason and
gravity neither existed nor extrapolated

therefore time sauntered and gathered
our singular reminiscence

And in thou ocular prisms
in the midst of colour and truth
where unfolded beauty lay

Ye irises yield sheer pulchritude
akin to grey storms, whereto
a passion play ensues, betwixt
embers warmth and hue
whereas logic hath no rule

Ye beguiled. simply but ushered
forth my heartfelt lay
to which I hath not ever discoursed
by quill nor faculty
until this day

Thou beget thee anew

We

I gander at you, and you
aren't far from me_
we are the same page
and the same self tone
on music sheets that
never end
We are wings
that share branches
and take to the air_
never unpaired
We are the closeness
between two lovers_
that cry out
between two sheets
woven together clasp
We are like
an analogy from old_
that sums up
and defines everything
lest we say alas
We are like two springs
spaking into two rivers
and flowing from
two different continents
but our outfall shares

the same ocean
We are sounds
that travel at the same distance
because our utterance
of jovial captivation
leaps from the same lungs
and they breath common
terms of endearments
into ears that understand
the same love song
I would love to
awaken every morn
and see you anew
in all your glory
and make love
to our heartfelt story
I would simply title it
'We' because we make
a great story

Dear Vagabond

You travel to and fro, the dance of the weary
your ravaged mind, weeps because chemical
imbalance, paints vivid colors but does not
bring you joy_

Your feet are visibly sore
Reaching into what mankind toils for

Soft leather, jammed in pockets by hurried hands
hard plastics bearing quasi-personal data

you've known once before, who you were but
could no longer provide_

I am beside myself to aide you
you utter despair on the hot pavement
where trees cast shadows of scantly clad
shaded relief

The other blood-red American's continue
hurriedly past because house values just
went down

You are quite the clash and the law will
soon be afoot, because busy hands on
touchscreens have hasty plans for your
demise

Sustenance is purposeful but dream
American, the golden arches you, plea with a
smile most childlike_

A gleam amidst the iris of yellowed eyes
are you economically or are you, bedazzled
by falsehoods like everyday people_

I see commonality

Three tedious years, you have been bereft
of your sanity and all you do is dream of water
this Arizona Sun takes no prisoners
it's far more cruel than society_

Implore I, of you, are you a functioning addict
like Hollywood debutantes and wall street wives
but instead, you were cast aside-_

Does your vice soak life into your life or pain
into your hell_

You will never tell the likes of me
your testimony is silent like Elephants caged
in meager rooms, under the big top_

All can see

The greenbacks do not matter because
I ventured close enough just to speak
my vice into your life_

God bless you...
and your reply is blink like unused canvases
He is however, an omnipotent ink

Sincerely,
Vagabond, I

Grief Literature

As one sits
pondering on
the animate and
inanimate

One knows
the same decomposers
break every living thing
down

Every living thing
which is earthly gone.
Gone or passed
in the self-same tone

I witnessed a shooting
star
the other day
gone, so far away

I understood you
Sparrow
for you were
with song

You sang me
a little ditty
Ravens crowed
in envy

Only replaying
me one scene
where human hope
beams and dies

The vultures gather
as always, while
we tinker by like
grief stricken dolls

their eyes cast
not by any remorse
they've witnessed
an ocean of tears

and time saunters
on while one is
buried live, emotive
logic is a sultry coffin

trapped in meager
rooms like the
other Jane's and
John's

Not to fret
one has their
deepest sympathies
and grief literature

I digress

Betwixt reality
and a foreign land
should I caress your crown
or hold your hand

as you lie
there where machines
mock life, where
false human hope

beamed forth
like some mad
dream, I am
still pondering

The words
grief literature

Reflections at the Red Light

Although, we discourse emotively

beseeching, that which is a given

though, I cannot possibly emote because my heartfelt lay

is somehow with unsound skeletal mishaps

My faculties pause and refrain

melodious is the threnody beguiling forgiveness within mute hearts

There is no duality here for thou art my beloved

Yet, in all my humanness, I hear the bleating of those to whom

thou dost dine upon

I cannot muster to doll up my compunction for it is no beauty queen

There is a great sentry that does not allow me to emote from the sleeve

giving no pardons to those garbed as sheep

Telephonically thou reaches thee without flowers

uttering pure love

Mortality has visited thee, confronted thee

sauntering betwixt the shore of your innate ability

to bask in hatred

What dirge ebbs at thee soul

Revisit thee with pain, for it begets more pain

Our blood brethren acted upon murder of the self

So, we've arrived at differing shores of life expectancy

and decided to love one another amidst the guttural

but heartfelt laugh, jar

Where commonality resides within the esophagus

there is a certain bile that gives way to truth

swallowed out of anatomical programming

but digested by way of ulcerative hearts

Suicide is but a fallacy, a mimicry of permanency

dressed up in moments where silent silhouettes waltz

to deaths rattle, where the clamoring of drums drive

Pained souls to venture into the deep

where those left behind, rebuild ones blunder

forever piecing together the remnants of a befuddling demise

Let's not ruminate nor labor where capable light
sheds truth

tis to vanity

The Duality of the Wolf

Two sides of moon
We guttural despair unto each

Calling unto night
We the derelicts amidst moonlight

Two sides of man
We guttural despair unto each

Calling unto sight
We the instruments unto night

Two sides unto innermost
We greedily feed unto each

Calling unto within
We balance unto sin

Two sides unto win
We murder unto oneself

Calling unto our duality
We can only, defeat unto self

Greer

Frost bespeaks of snow
For they're not quasi-alike
They're both endeavored upon
for the Crow shook down upon
Both, flitting to and fro
disturbing the scene
Dusting the atmosphere with
mirth and to whom, do they owe
solstice

Let us Journey

Bespeak me, a ballad
for it hath been, a month of Sunday's

If only, we were atemporal
for it hath been, a night of many moons

Would time, ebb as timeless rivers
for overtime, water is the iron that shapes

Shall constructs, be murdered haplessly
for overtime, our mental capacities bloom

Saunter with me, amidst the primroses
for our, human experience leaves impressions

Saunter with me, on winters' solstice
for we shall, meander the sands of time

One Line, You

The broad strokes of my quill depict you and
you remain my most desirable instrument.

Laid Bare

They say, poetry is another kind of intimacy
bones laid bare
Lyrically we dissect and formulate your marrow
bones laid bare
Intricately traversing the anomalies known as
you
bones laid bare
Lexicons to diaphragms, we whisper to breath,
you
bones laid bare

Said of Blues

Every utterance leads to a silhouette of a
wakeful nightmare
Why else do we drown in whiskey and ambient
light
Whilst brass percussions propagate and prove us
melancholy
and discourse our hurt, ever so vividly

One Line, Means Well

Potentiality is a dolled up carcass, without action.

Question

There in your voice, questionable fear
You want to know, if I, too hear it
When I ask_ when will you rationalize the
gapping
wound in your reality
The palpable and tangible wound.

Nowhere Safe

Today, I met a lady
my desire was to formulate her in words
but I lacked verbosity because her pain was
immutable
her voice was like velvet curtains, despite tears
in her reality

Her poise was not hunched
her silver tresses bespoke of her youth
yesteryear bespoke of her loneliness and
the bygone times were etched in her clay

Her demeanor was so delicate
and deliberate but Alice chased white rabbits
and mad hatter's only brought her more pain
so, my thoughts meandered because

Tombstones are ever animated
until, they are dead
I was slain by her truth_
unsaid

www.ingramcontent.com/pod-product-compliance
Lightning Source LLC
Chambersburg PA
CBHW051745130826
49812CB00033B/1013
9789395890168